michael
graves

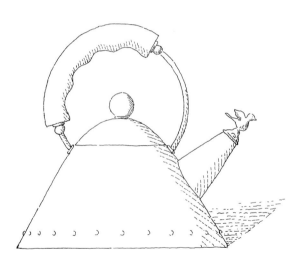

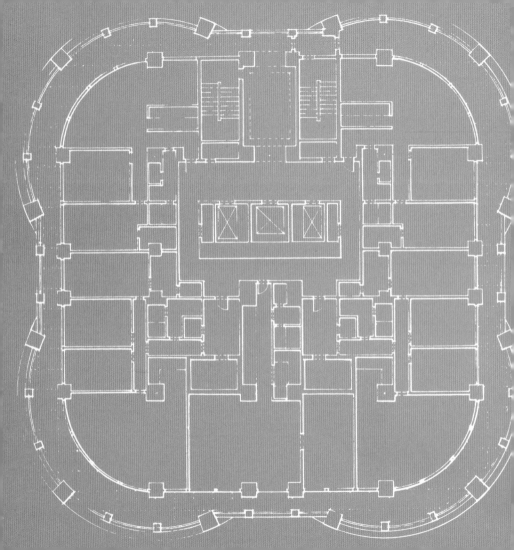

COMPACT DESIGN PORTFOLIO

michael
graves

BY   JULIE IOVINE

EDITED BY   MARISA BARTOLUCCI + RAUL CABRA

CHRONICLE BOOKS

SAN FRANCISCO

Text copyright © 2002
by Julie Iovine.

Design by Raul Cabra and Maxine Ressler
for Cabra Diseño, San Francisco.

Library of Congress Cataloging-
in-Publication Data available.

ISBN 0-8118-3251-1

Manufactured in China

Distributed in Canada
by Raincoast Books
9050 Shaughnessy Street
Vancouver, British Columbia V6P 6E5

10 9 8 7 6 5 4 3 2 1

Chronicle Books LLC
85 Second Street
San Francisco, California 94105
www.chroniclebooks.com

FRONT COVER: TOASTER FOR TARGET, 1999

BACK COVER: TEA KETTLE FOR ALESSI, 1985

PAGES 1 AND 3: SKETCH AND TEA KETTLE FOR ALESSI, 1985

PAGE 2: BLUEPRINT FOR PORTSIDE APARTMENT TOWER,
YOKOHAMA, JAPAN, 1982–89

PAGE 6: PORTSIDE APARTMENT TOWER, YOKOHAMA, JAPAN,
1988–92

ACKNOWLEDGMENTS

Thanks to Caroline Hancock and Courtney Havran at the Michael Graves studio, who embraced this project with enthusiasm from the beginning, and were always there to answer questions no matter how trivial. Our appreciation extends to everyone else on the Michael Graves team who assisted in researching and assembling the images that make up this book. We appreciate, too, the fine skill that Maxine Ressler brought to the book's design, and Michael Jao's professional production work. We are also grateful to Chronicle's designer Vivien Sung, for trusting us aesthetically and encouraging our play. Particular thanks go to our terrific editor at Chronicle, Alan Rapp, who early on championed the idea of this series. Alan was always at hand with sound editorial and design advice and good humor.

PHOTO CREDITS

Alessi
pp. 51, 52–53, 60, 61, 67

Marek Bulaj
pp. 62, 78, 89, 91, 92, 93

Dorsey Collection
p. 38

Susan Gilmore
pp. 36–37, 40, 86

Michael Graves & Associates
pp. 1, 3, 12, 13, 16 (kettle), 16 (salt and pepper shaker), 23, 26–27, 32, 33, 35, 39, 41, 44–45, 48, 54–55, 56, 57, 58, 59, 64, 65, 69 (sketch), 71, 72, 73, 74, 77, 79, 80, 81 (all), 82, 83, 84, 85, 88, 90

Tim Hursley
pp. 24, 30

Isau Inbe
p. 6

Bill Phelps
p. 42

Sadamu Saitu
p. 29

Steuben
p. 73

T & E
p. 31

William Taylor
pp. 16 (French press), 16 (chair), 28, 49, 50, 54, 63, 66, 70

Michael Graves

Designer as Populist   By Julie Iovine

Michael Graves, architect, artist, product designer, and enigma. Though he may have been dismissed as a Postmodern has-been by the architectural elite, he is a household name. Indeed, he is the first modern architect to get the full celebrity treatment (Frank Lloyd Wright behaved like a rock star, but Graves was voted *GQ* Man of the Year in 1999). This broad appeal has rendered him something of a curiosity within the architectural profession. He flourishes on his own terms.

The man himself is a bit of a mystery as well. Few architects pay closer attention to domestic issues, whether designing objects for the home or collecting with meticulous connoisseurship for his own. Yet his personal brand of domesticity is a solitary one. The sixty-six-year-old architect lives by himself, a black Labrador his most constant companion. Professionally, Graves has created a world unto itself and welcomed the real world to partake of it. Whether designing a singing tea kettle or a vast complex of domes and vaults for a village resort in Egypt, Graves's distinctly personal language derives from things that while close to home also resonate with the ages.

He has achieved the dream of every architect—the chance to place his stamp on just about everything in sight. Rarely do architects ever get the opportunity to design even a few one-of-a-kind furnishings or precious objects lined on a high-priced shelf unless commissioned by a wealthy, indulgent client. Michael Graves has designed thousands of products both humble and exquisite, enough to make any designer question the breadth of his or her own aspirations. **"I never thought you did anything else but it all,"** says Graves matter-of-factly. **"I never drew the line anywhere."**

Graves's present popularity parallels the resurgence of contemporary design among the public. Seen as both desirable and attainable thanks to a strong economy, it has attracted a new generation of enthusiasts weaned on computers and the notion that any barrier between architecture and design is purely arbitrary. Michael Graves, pen and paintbrush in hand, preceded this belief by decades. And any future consideration of millennial design will have to reckon with his impact.

It is hard to imagine that he planned it that way. Born in Indianapolis on July 9, 1934, Graves is the son of a livestock broker and a nurse. He grew up in the small-town America made mythological in the pom-pom optimism of early Judy Garland and Mickey Rooney movies. As a boy, Graves loved to draw, but his mother pointed out that being an artist was an awfully hard way to make a living. "She suggested that I think of being an engineer or architect instead," Graves recalls. Her description of what engineers do did not impress him, however. Graves retorted, "Then, I'll be an architect," and immediately started making sketches of the houses in his neighborhood.

In high school, Graves took the only classes offered in architectural rendering, and he took them again when no new ones were available. He won a statewide drawing contest for his illustration of the Parthenon. The prize was a set of drawing pens that the architect still has. "You can't imagine how it felt," says Graves of that early endorsement. "It was like winning the Olympics. It was a blessing no parent can give you."

His course was set. Graves went on to study architecture at the University of Cincinnati and then at Harvard, where he received his master's degree in 1959.

His horizons expanded further when he won the Prix de Rome, enabling him to spend two years at the American Academy. It was a profound experience. In Italy, he was exposed to some of the most powerful architecture ever built, while at the same time, he became immersed in a genial way of living that proved utterly seductive to the Midwestern boy.

Upon his return to the United States, Graves became a professor of architecture at Princeton University, a position he retains today. His earliest jobs were small renovations for neighbors in Princeton, among them one for the friends of his then in-laws. ("I was just the boy next door," he quips.) This was a kitchen addition to a 1930s Cape Cod. Its exaggerated geometries and vinyl tile flooring in shifting grids and colors earned Graves the nickname "the Cubist Kitchen King."

At that time, in the early sixties, the modern architecture movement had lost its vigor. Young architects like Graves and his fellow teachers in Princeton—Peter Eisenman and Richard Meier—were restless. There was a revolutionary spirit in the air, and they wanted to be part of it. The vast corporate-sponsored cereal boxes that passed for new architecture were not for them. The three friends joined two other architects—Charles Gwathmey, who was also teaching at Princeton, and John Heyduk, who was at New York's Cooper Union—to talk about their work, which sought to reinvigorate Modernism, and return it to the intellectual rigor and aesthetic purism of their hero, Le Corbusier. The group would become known as the New York Five and their informal sessions, held at the Museum of Modern Art, would become legendary among students of architecture, especially after the book *New York Five* was published in 1972, documenting their early architectural projects. Typically, Graves demurs when asked about those heady days. "We just thought we were being anonymous," he says.

There is a Zelig-like flow to Graves's career. He keeps reemerging before the public as renegade Modernist, then Postmodernist kingpin, then populist product designer. His membership in the New York Five, however, was relatively brief. Also known as the Whites, it was roundly skewered in Tom Wolfe's diatribe against Modernism, *From Bauhaus to Our House*. Graves was the first to break ranks. **"I wanted my language to be more accessible and contextual,"** says the architect now. Not surprisingly, he accomplished this goal with drawings the likes of which no one had seen before— a series of moody, Cubist-inspired elemental sketches of buildings in saturated colors on yellow tracing paper that instantly became collector's items. The British critic Rowen Moore, recalling the days when Graves's originality made him a cult figure among architecture students around the world, said that "Anyone who went to America would bring back rolls of the translucent yellow paper that Graves drew on, and would treasure them."

Indeed, Graves's drawings are often credited with creating the 1980s rage for collecting architectural works on paper. Graves's intensely personal rediscovery of the poetic and the figurative in architecture became bound up in a new movement being heralded in the late 1970s and early 1980s as Postmodernism. While other architects delved into their encyclopedias to dredge up historical models to copy, Graves, in the words of the architect Robert A. M. Stern, dean of the Yale School of Architecture, **"remained committed to a uniquely personal, even at times ironic, vision of Classicism."** Indeed, no matter the scale, Graves's projects have a sense of humor and irony. Graves likes to anthropomorphize. His buildings have heads and feet, or at the very least tops and bottoms. His products sometimes smile. Ever the humanist, Graves is hard put to explain his ironic gestures, and says simply, "I guess I just don't take life that seriously." The remark underscores a certain aloofness that is part of Graves's persona. While the colleagues of his New York Five days have all remained good friends, they rarely hobnob in public. Princeton, though only an hour away from Manhattan, is both Graves's home and his ivory tower.

His first major public commission, the 1982 Portland Office Building, created a sensation that catapulted him to national fame and controversy. His drawings of various unbuilt projects, like his initial sketches for the Portland building, were already well known and admired. And now he was building. Expectations were enormously high, and they were dashed quickly when the decorations and color that looked so luscious on paper were thought by many not to translate well onto a large scale. Herbert Muschamp, the architecture critic of the *New York Times,* describes the building as "some grotesque architectural version of Alice after she telescopes out into the giant of Wonderland." Adorned with intensely colored swags and keystones and, possibly, a grimacing face on one wall, the Portland Building is both loved and loathed. It has become an indelible icon of the city and of the frivolity of 1980s Postmodernism.

The controversy didn't hurt his career. For the rest of the decade, Graves was the odds-on favorite for every prominent architectural commission in the country. In short order he was hired to design the Humana headquarters building in Louisville, Kentucky (listed in *Time* magazine as one of the ten best buildings of the 1980s); the Newark Museum in New Jersey; the Phoenix Municipal Government Center in Arizona; the Clos

Pegase Winery in Napa Valley, California; and the San Juan Capistrano Library in San Juan Capistrano, California, a modestly scaled reinterpretation of California Mission style through a Tuscan lens that many believe to be his most sensitive building. The heavily monumental addition he proposed for the Whitney Museum of American Art in New York, however, was permanently scuttled.

But it was his designs for the Disney Company that showed a wider audience what a total work by Michael Graves could be. The 1986 Team Disney Building, a corporate headquarters in Burbank, California, boldly combined the Classical and the comical. Its Parthenon-like pediment is held aloft by nineteen-foot dwarves. In this instance, irony and corporate identity romped happily to the altar. Disney then hired Graves to design hotels for Disney World in Orlando, Florida. With their gigantic forty-seven-foot namesakes astride their roofs like modern-day colossi, the Dolphin and the Swan Hotels are monuments to good humor. "Michael raised the bar on hotel design," says Stern, a fellow alum in designing high-profile architecture for the Disney Company. **"Suddenly those dumb ordinary boxes were no longer possible for anyone wishing to cater to a certain crowd. They had to have a presence, a story, and be witty."**

Nor are these hotels the empty shells of a design architect who then turns the interiors over to an associated firm for completion. Graves designed every wallpaper, rug,

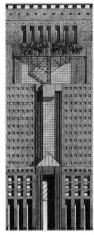

MAIN STREET ELEVATION
FOR THE HUMANA
BUILDING, LOUISVILLE,
KENTUCKY, 1982–85

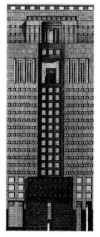

SOUTH ELEVATION FOR THE HUMANA BUILDING, LOUISVILLE, KENTUCKY, 1982–85

palm planter, and plate. Inside the Dolphin, the lobby ceiling is tented, the columns are fluted like papyrus, and the walls are covered in murals and stripes. The inevitable long corridors, so stifling in any other large hotel, are enlivened by murals of life-size beach scenes; the doors look like cabana flaps, and the furniture in the guest rooms is festooned with pineapples and palm trees. In the *New York Times,* architecture critic Paul Goldberger described the two hotels as "extravagant, flamboyant works of decoration, willfully eccentric and dazzlingly entertaining," but he went on to wonder if they aren't perhaps too knowing and ironic for the simple, themed pleasures of Disney World.

Nonetheless, the Dolphin and the Swan provided Graves with the opportunity to do it all, and in his own style. But it was not the first time that Graves had expressed an interest in expanding the role of architect. In the early 1980s he started to design for Sunar Hauserman, an office furniture manufacturer based in Cleveland. He calls that early commission serendipitous, and his attitude toward it "nervy." "I had absolutely no work at the time, but I was still real ballsy," he says, with his usual combination of diffidence and candor. "I told Bobby Cadwallader [president of Sunar] that I'd do the showrooms if he'd let me do the furniture, too. And he said to me, 'Listen, Michael, first do the showrooms and if they're a success then you can do the furniture.'" Graves not only went on to do the design, but also the furniture.

Graves also collaborated with the flamboyant Italian design group Memphis on a few furniture pieces that combined refined craftsmanship with puckish good humor. His 1981 Plaza dressing table was made of natural briar with blue drawers and a dunce cap pyramid perched on a blank mirror face surrounded by shimmering glass tiles. The Plaza vanity is an early example of a favorite Graves hybrid: furniture that looks like architecture that looks like a person, or in this case, a robot.

However, the promise shown by the architect's product design work with Disney and Memphis could not have anticipated the extraordinary success of his association with Alessi, the Italian product manufacturer, that began around 1980. **The sterling silver tea service—a squat fluted body with blue Bakelite balls for feet—that he designed in 1982 is most often cited as the fork in the road for Graves. After** **that, he would never again be known as primarily an architect.** By 1994, there were six people in his office working exclusively on products. And by millennium's end, he had designed well over a thousand different objects, from Etruscan-inspired cuff links made with precious stones to a chrome toilet paper holder shaped like a squiggle.

Graves himself is nonplussed by all those who wonder how an architect can design more than just buildings. "I don't know when architects decided to surrender the interiors to others. I suppose it was after World War II," he says, a gentle dig perhaps at other architects of his generation who seem satisfied to design only exteriors, leaving interior decorators to take over the inside. Before then, Graves is quick to point out, architects did it all. In fact, he himself remembers as a young man making a pilgrimage to the offices of Eero Saarinen, where he saw the famed Tulip chair on the working boards. "I grew up in architecture school in the 1950s, when our heroes were Saarinen, who did a lot of furniture, and Charles Eames, who was making movies, furniture, everything. He was really King of the Hill." Indeed, after receiving his master's, Graves spent a year in the office of George Nelson, the furniture designer and creative director for Herman Miller who was also a photographer, graphic designer, and editor. Through Nelson, Graves became familiar with the work of the Eameses, and especially of Alexander Girard, whose use of brilliant color inspired by the Southwest and Central America surely influenced Graves's own interest in color.

Graves didn't hesitate when he was approached by Alberto Alessi who, with a marketing gimmick in mind, had also tapped a dozen or so other prominent architects, including Richard Meier, Robert A. M. Stern, Aldo Rossi, and Arata Isozaki. While well known in Italy, Alessi wanted to be an important presence in America, too. So he commissioned the architects to design one-of-a-kind tea services that, rather than being hawked in stores, were put on display in museums and galleries, like the Metropolitan Museum of Art and Max Protetch in New York. **Even Alessi was surprised when Graves's $25,000 tea service began to sell** (at least 40 in the first blush of introduction!). The company came back to Graves and asked him to design a moderate-priced tea kettle expressly for an American audience. (The Italian manufacturer believed that Americans made a lot of instant coffee.)

In the first go-round, the architect had been extended carte blanche to make art, but now he was expected to deliver a tea kettle that was rigorously practical. It had to boil water quickly, be easy to lift when full, and take gas heat without getting its spout burnt. Graves wanted the tea kettle to be whimsical, too. He was in good company, as many Alessi products have a cartoonish quality. And so Graves gave his kettle a whistle in the shape of a red bird spout that sings when the water comes to a boil. Ironic, charming, and efficient, the Singing Bird tea kettle, as it's known, hit a nerve; Graves had created yet another icon of the 1980s.

Alessi quickly commissioned Graves to do more. **"All my designers have at least a few failures, but not Michael,"** Alberto Alessi has said of his experience with architects designing products. "All his stuff sells." Consistency, it seems, is the architect's strong suit. Graves himself says his approach is the same whether he is designing a building or a kettle. In both he aims for an easily recognizable relationship between person and thing. "You think about how you're going to put your hand on the grip of a kettle in the same way that you think about the placement of your hand on the pull of a door," he says.

Many architects are practical; Graves is enthusiastic about common objects with common uses. And where other architects might condescend to design a few precious keepsakes, Graves will try anything. He's designed sets and costumes for the Joffrey Ballet and even a shopping bag for Bloomingdale's; the latter won him a generous round of criticism for being an undignified use of his talent. Graves has been able to work more freely in Europe and Asia, where the professional split between architec-

ture and design is not so rigid. Throughout the 1980s and early 1990s, most of his commissions for products came from abroad. He designed precious jewelry for Cleto Munari of Milan; mass-produced rugs with stylized floral motifs for Vorwerk of Germany; chairs for Sawaya Moroni, also of Milan; and vinyl flooring for the Japanese company Tajima.

In all his products, there are recognizable themes—a sense of the human body, an appeal to the emotions, and an element of ceremony and storytelling. Born of a deep appreciation for the traditions of classical humanism, Graves's products have personalities. They reach out to be touched, to be enjoyed, to be bought and taken home. But it takes more than that to get things made. Graves thoroughly understands the nuts and bolts of production. "People will come to me with a chair they want made," Graves says. "They don't realize it doesn't work like that. You have to know about much more than just design. Everything has to be designed to make it possible for anyone to assemble. Even symmetry, for instance, can be a problem. You may think the front and the back are obvious, but when something arrives from Malaysia, knocked down in a box, and has to be assembled in the back room at Target, then you'd better make sure that all the screws only work in one direction."

As always, Graves pays attention to the little things. In fact, the small canvas of the home attracts him more than anything else. His appreciation for the domestic things in life has only increased with age. Recalling those early years in Italy, the architect explains that he learned then about the intimate connection between people and the things that surround them. "It sounds kind of sappy," he says, "but at this point in my life, it has become more meaningful than ever for me to make places for people to be together. And that means all the stuff that goes with it. I'm interested not just in making the house, but the garden, and the garden table, and the chairs that people use to sit around the table, and the plates on the table, too. Others might want to design; I want to make things livable, without compromises."

His own home is a laboratory "filled with all the things I care about," he says. Set in a quiet, residential neighborhood in Princeton, the house suggests the sand-blasted essence of an Italian villa. Graves calls it "the Warehouse" because that is what it was when it was built in the 1920s by Italian masons imported to work on campus buildings. Its transformation has been gradual and absolute. Once a furniture repository, it now has formal gardens with espaliered plants clinging to its plastered walls and wisteria twining around its columns. Tall, narrow doors give access to an interior that flows effortlessly from circular entry to barrel-vaulted niches and open galleries with thick columns. Architecture critic Jan Abrams has called Graves's home, together with his nearby office, "a Palladian agricultural estate."

But in its intricacies and pleasures (miniature ionic columns support the shelves in the library), it recalls as well the 1811 home of Sir John Soane, the architect of the Bank of England. The house is a connoisseur's dream. Every surface is a display place; every piece of furniture carefully curated. Recently, Graves admitted that for years he would put products of his own design only in the kitchen, and nowhere else in the house. Asked why, he answered nonchalantly that he simply hadn't found the right fit. He finally did introduce a couple of chairs he had designed for a Hyatt hotel in La Jolla to his living room, only larger than the originals. He does, however, use the Singing Bird tea kettle from Alessi and the toaster from Target every morning. Elsewhere, the furniture consists of Beidermeier and Deco pieces picked up over thirty years of collecting neoclassically inspired styles.

As befitting the villa of some Italian count of ancient lineage, the library is extensive. Graves's dog is always somewhere underfoot. The architect's Midwestern roots are buried deep and his personal collections are esoteric. They include a vase he bought for five dollars when studying in Rome along with his first serious acquisitions, two Baroque drawings. Over the years, his tastes—and buying power—have expanded to include Wedgewood, seventeenth-century engravings, nineteenth-century French bronzes, and most curiously, nineteenth-century ink wells shaped like the Temple of Vesta in Rome. He prefers things, he says, that have "the ability to age with interest."

Graves's love of color sets him apart from other architects of his generation, who tend to tread timidly beyond a spectrum ranging from silver to white and black. He applies color with bold conviction. The combination of rust-toned terra-cottas, mustardy ochres, and cerulean blues have become part of the architect's signature. Recurring in his paintings as well as his buildings, they create their own world, part Tuscan landscape, part Egyptian tomb, part Arcadian dream. The architect's use of robin's egg blue has become as much a part of his signature as his handwritten name.

In his buildings, color allows the architecture to emerge from the landscape as if it were actually a part of it. Earthbound reds give way to cream as the upper stories shade toward the paler hues of the sky. In his products, color adds to the upbeat mood. What could be more cheerful than a blue toaster? Aldo Rossi, the Italian architect, once quipped that Graves's objects are so appealing to people because they "create a happy world."

In 1994, Graves opened up the Graves Design Store in Princeton, a tiny 250-square-foot space dedicated to his collected designs. Without precedence among well-known architects, this small retail operation, according to Graves, is mostly a convenience for all the people who formerly tracked down his office staff with inquiries about where to get the architect's designs. After all, by now, he has worked with over fifty different manufacturers. At the store, shelves are loaded with watches, jewelry, frames, and leather goods, as well as note cards and calendars printed with Graves's landscape paintings and his architecture. The many clocks are all set at ten minutes past ten, because Graves likes them to appear to be smiling. He has rejected the notion that the shop might expand into a national chain; for one thing, the name "Graves" has already spread coast to coast through his work for Target.

Shortly before Graves opened his shop, he said in interviews that he still thought of the products he designed as individual commissions. He did not anticipate a relationship with a mass-market retailer, nor did he appear to strive for one. In keeping with his diffident personality, Graves hasn't courted the people, but populism has found him out. His liaison with Target began when the budget retailer hired the architect to design a construction fence protecting the Washington Monument during its restoration. Target was the primary sponsor, donating $6 million to the project.

Graves devised a Christo-like sheath upon which were etched the exaggerated outlines of the building's own bricks. It looked stupendous at night, both shielding the 555-foot monument and celebrating the extraordinary fact of its stone construction. Blair Kamen, the architecture critic for the *Chicago Tribune,* described Graves's scaffolding design as having "the felicitous effect of taking a familiar object and transforming it into something fresh and contemporary."

Target returned to Graves for more. "The monument project was so successful and the chemistry was so good," says Bob Guelich, a senior vice-president at Target. **"Our interests collided. He wanted his message to reach a broader audience, and we wanted to elevate our position among our customers."** In January 1999, the Graves collection for Target was introduced, including a spatula, an ice-cream scoop, a potato peeler, a toaster, and a tea kettle with a red whistle for a spout. For the blue spatula, Graves chose Santoprene, the latest development in durable, flexible rubber. "We now call it 'Target blue' in the office," says Graves. Within a year, Graves had put his name to over five hundred items, including mop buckets, a cordless telephone, and a coffeemaker.

The best-selling Graves product so far is a toilet brush, according to Guelich. "It's a popular product anyway," he says, "but no one has ever given people a good design option before." The architect's success at reaching the widest imaginable audience has forced critics who had ceased paying close attention to him in the aftermath of Postmodernism to sit up and take notice. **"Allowing that the democratization of design is the great design story of the late twentieth century,"** says Paul Goldberger, reviewing Graves's career, **"Michael is the only architect who has chosen to take a fully active role in that movement, not only participating, but shaping its direction."** In the Graves collection for Target, prices rarely exceed a hundred dollars, but the architect's signature is as clear as ever. His forms are still often anthropomorphic, if not with head and feet, then with a definite personality, as in the Bakelite steak knife with a shark's grin blade.

If sex sells cars, then when it comes to housewares, a dose of wit can inspire intense product loyalty, Graves has discovered. He says that he must set aside an hour or so every week to autograph the toasters, chess sets, kettles, books, and posters that are sent in by fans. But the ultimate compliment, he says, is when people tell him that they not only appreciate how his things work, but, more importantly to him, "They always add, 'and it makes me smile.'" Achieving the highest degree of humanity and humor is not only the standard by which Graves defines his success (after all, profitability came easily), it has become the standard of design that his public now expects.

MIRAMAR RESORT HOTEL, EL GOUNA, EGYPT,
1995–97

There is a Zelig-like flow to his career, first renegade Modernist, then Postmodernist kingpin, then populist product designer. In the early 1970s, he broke ranks with his avant-garde modernist colleagues. "I wanted my language to be more accessible and contextual," he explains. Not surprisingly, he accomplished this goal with drawings the likes of which no one had seen before—moody, Cubist-inspired elemental sketches of buildings in saturated colors on yellow tracing paper that instantly became collector's items.

WESTERN HISTORY READING ROOM, DENVER
CENTRAL LIBRARY, DENVER, COLORADO, 1990–91

FOLLOWING PAGES: COMPETITION DRAWING
FOR PROPOSED ARTS CENTER AT OHIO STATE
UNIVERSITY, 1983

Ohio State University
center for the visual arts
Phase I

FINESTRA CHAIR FOR VECTA AI, 1989

KASUMI RESEARCH AND TRAINING CENTER,
TSUKUBA, JAPAN, 1990–94

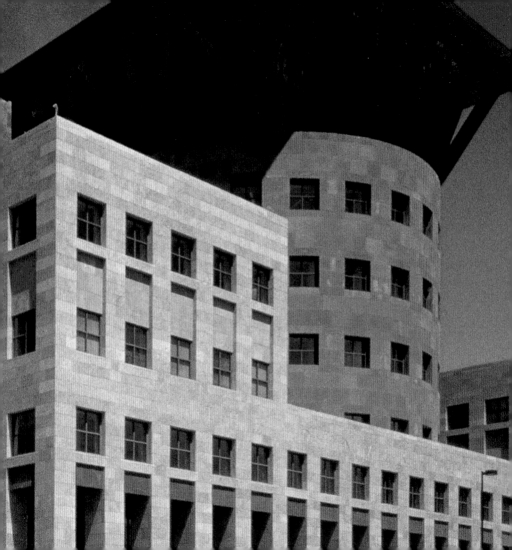

OCULUS CHAIR FOR VECTA AI, 1989

CLOCK FOR ALESSI, 1992
TABLE STUDIES, 1977–81

CERAMIC VASE FOR SWID POWELL, 1989

CARPET DESIGN FOR VORWERK'S DIALOG
COLLECTION, 1987

Few architects pay as close attention to domestic issues as Graves. Whether designing a singing tea kettle or a vast complex of domes and vaults for a village resort in Egypt, Graves's distinctly personal language derives from things that while close to home also resonate with the ages.

DINING ROOM, CEDAR GABLES HOUSE, MINNETONKA, MINNESOTA, 1999

ARMCHAIRS FOR THE DORSEY COLLECTION, 1990

DREAMSCAPE BATHROOM FIXTURES FOR
DURAVIT, 1999

Many architects are practical; Graves is enthusiastic about common objects with common uses. And where other architects might condescend to design a few precious keepsakes, Graves will try anything. He's designed sets and costumes for the Joffrey Ballet and even a shopping bag for Bloomingdale's.

MICHAEL GRAVES OUTSIDE HIS HOME, 1998

PROGRAMMA 6 SILVER COFFEE AND TEA SET
FOR ALESSI, 1982

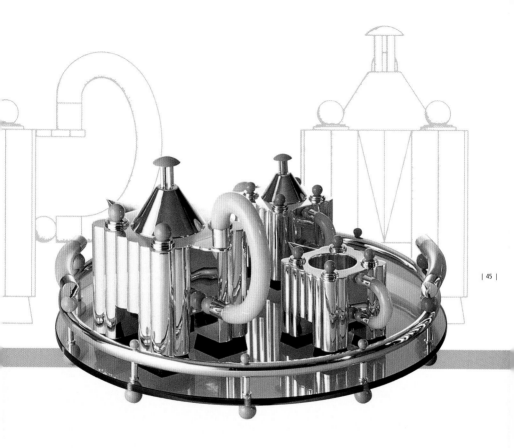

TEA KETTLE FOR ALESSI, 1985

RIGHT: SKETCH FOR TAIWAN NATIONAL MUSEUM
OF PRE-HISTORY

Graves was expected by Alessi to deliver a tea kettle that was rigorously practical. It had to boil water quickly, be easy to lift when full, and take gas heat without getting its spout burnt. Graves wanted the tea kettle to be whimsical, too. So he gave it a whistle in the shape of a red bird spout that sings when the water comes to a boil. Ironic, charming, and efficient, the Singing Bird tea kettle hit a nerve; Graves had created yet another icon of the 1980s.

CREAM PITCHER AND SUGAR BOWL
FOR ALESSI, 1987

| 49 |

PEPPER MILL AND SALT SHAKER
FOR ALESSI, 1987

| 51 |

FOLLOWING PAGES: FAMILY OF PRODUCTS
FOR ALESSI, 1984–94

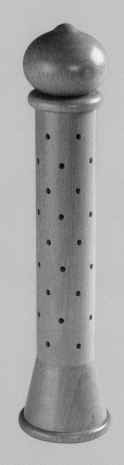

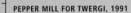PEPPER MILL FOR TWERGI, 1991

EUCLID PLASTICWARE FOR ALESSI, 1993

EUCLID PLASTICWARE FOR ALESSI, 1993

GLASS-COVERED CHEESE PLATE FOR ALESSI, 1997

CLOCK FOR ALESSI, 1992

WRISTWATCHES FOR MARKUSE, 1992

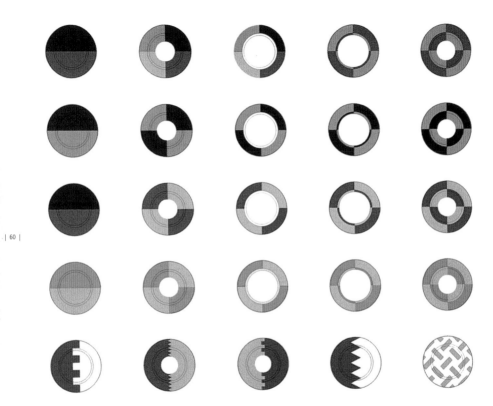

POSTER OF PLATE STUDY FOR ALESSI, 1997 DINNERWARE FOR ALESSI, 1997

GLASS TEAPOT WITH TEA BALL FOR LEONARDO,
2000

BIG DIPPER COFFEEPOT AND SERVICE FOR
SWID POWELL, 1986–87

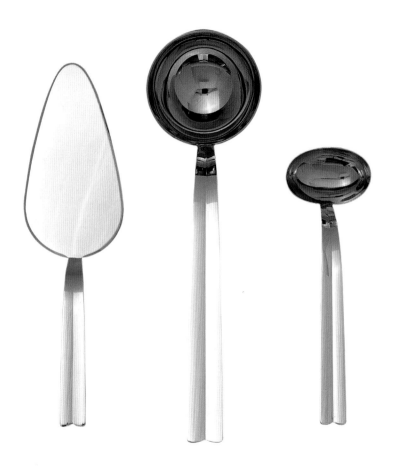

SILVER FLATWARE FOR ALESSI, 1994

BREADBOX FOR ALESSI, 1994

CRUET STAND FOR ALESSI, 1994

Graves has achieved the dream of every architect—the chance to place his stamp on just about everything in sight. He has designed thousands of products both humble and exquisite, enough to make any designer question the breadth of his or her own aspirations. "I never thought you did anything else but it all," he says matter-of-factly. "I never drew the line anywhere."

CHARM BRACELET FOR BELVEDERE STUDIO, 1991

WRISTWATCH FOR CLETO MUNARI, 1985

RING FOR CLETO
MUNARI, 1985

VASES FOR STEUBEN, 1986–88

Graves is not afraid to be boldly populist, and so he eagerly agreed to work with the discount retail chain Target. So far he's designed more than five hundred products for the company. According to critic Paul Goldberger, his mass-market success has forced many architecture critics to once again sit up and take notice of his work. Graves, he believes, has lead in the democratization of design, which he calls "the great design story of the late twentieth century."

GRAVES WORKING IN HIS STUDY, 1995

TOILET BRUSH FOR TARGET, 1999

ILLUMINATED SCAFFOLDING FOR WASHINGTON
MONUMENT RESTORATION, 1998–2000

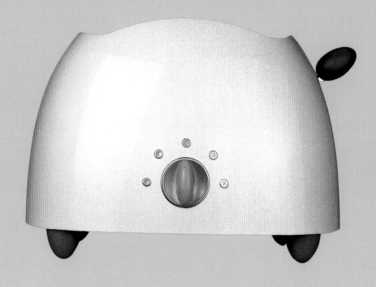

TOASTER FOR TARGET, 1999

TEA KETTLES FOR TARGET, 1999

BLENDER FOR TARGET, 1999

ICE BUCKET FOR TARGET, 1999

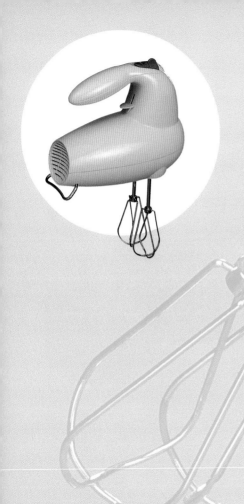

MIXER FOR TARGET, 1999

COOKWARE FOR TARGET, 2000

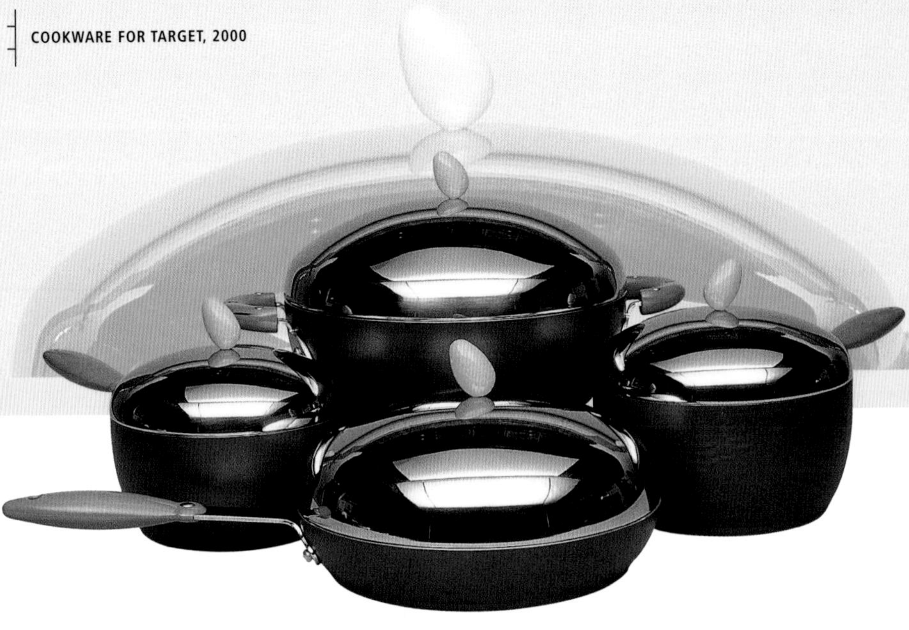

COOKING UTENSILS FOR TARGET, 2000

"It sounds kind of sappy," Graves says, "but at this point in my life, it has become more meaningful than ever for me to make places for people to be together. And that means all the stuff that goes with it. I'm interested not just in making the house, but the garden, and the garden table, and the chairs . . . and the plates on the table, too. Others might want to design; I want to make things livable, without compromises."

KITCHEN, CEDAR GABLES HOUSE, MINNETONKA, MINNESOTA, 1999

FLATWARE FOR TARGET, 2000

CHESS SET FOR TARGET, 2000

SCONCES FOR TARGET, 2000

CORDLESS PHONE FOR TARGET, 2000

CD HEADSET FOR TARGET, 2000

PHILIPS

CLOCK RADIO FOR TARGET, 2000

MICHAEL GRAVES BIOGRAPHY

1934   Born July 9th in Indianapolis, Indiana

1958   Graduates from the University of Cincinnati with a degree in architecture

1959   Receives MA in architecture from Harvard University

1960   Wins the Prix de Rome; studies at the American Academy in Rome until 1962

1972   *New York Five* published

1981   Creates furniture for Sunar Hauserman

1981   Designs Plaza dressing table for Italian design firm Memphis

1982   Completes Portland Office Building, Portland, Oregon

1982   Designs Programma 6 sterling silver tea service for Alessi

1982   Creates special edition Bloomingdale's shopping bag

1983   Completes San Juan Capistrano Library, San Juan Capistrano, California

1985   Completes Humana Building in Louisville, Kentucky

1985   Completes Phoenix Municipal Government Center, Phoenix, Arizona

1985   Designs Singing Bird tea kettle for Alessi

1986   Completes Team Disney corporate headquarters, Burbank, California

1987   Completes Clos Pegase Winery, Napa Valley, California

1987   Designs Big Dipper coffee pot and service for Swid Powell

1989   Completes Newark Museum, Newark, New Jersey

1989   Creates chair series for Vecta AI

1990	Completes Walt Disney World Swan and Dolphin Hotels in Orlando, Florida
1991	Completes Denver Central Library, Denver, Colorado
1992	Designs wristwatches for Markuse
1993	Designs Euclid plasticware for Alessi
1994	Opens Graves Design Store, Princeton, New Jersey
1998	Completes the Ministry of Culture, the Hague, Netherlands
1998	Designs scaffolding for Washington Monument restoration
1999	Receives National Medal of Arts
1999	Housewares line for Target introduced
1999	Completes the Cedar Gables house, Minnetonka, Minnesota
2001	Receives the AIA Gold Medal

INDEX